The Silly Lilies

By: Abby Crosk

To order additional copies of this book, contact:
Xlibris
1-888-795-4274
www.Xlibris.com
Orders@Xlibris.com

THE SILLY LILIES

by
Abby Craft

DEDICATION

· ·

This story would never have come to be
without all my favorite munchkins.
Thanks for the inspiration

Beck

Boston

Boyce

Cora

Lillie

Lucie

Sutton

Tobias

Victoria

. . . .

Hey where have you been?
Don't tell me, you were stuck in a lion's den.

The silly lilies are here and ready to play.
So please, don't make them wait all day.

They are ready to show you how silly they can be
So come on have a look see.

. . . .

This lily is so silly, so silly in fact,
That he took off his petals and
is now wearing a top hat,

. . . .

This lily is silly so silly in fact,
That she decided to grow upside down,
With her roots in the air and petals on
the ground,

. . . .

This lily is silly so silly in fact,
That she is now an acrobat.

．．．．．．．．．．．．．．．．．．．．．．．．．．．．．

This lily is actually a tree,
And this lily is a bee,
And this lily is not just one color but three.

．．．．．．．．．．．．．．．．．．．．．．．．．．．．

. . . .

These lilies are so very silly!!!
As you can plainly see,
But each one is special, wonderful, and unique.
Just like you and me.

. . . .

Printed in the United States
By Bookmasters